Bastards of the Reagan Era

Also by Reginald Dwayne Betts

Poetry:

Shahid Reads His Own Palm (2010)

Memoir:

A Question of Freedom: A Memoir of Learning, Survival, and Coming of Age in Prison (2009)

Bastards of the Reagan Era

Reginald Dwayne Betts

FOUR WAY BOOKS
TRIBECA

Please direct all inquiries to:
Editorial Office
Four Way Books
POB 535, Village Station
New York, NY 10014
www.fourwaybooks.com

Library of Congress Cataloging-in-Publication Data

Betts, Reginald Dwayne.
[Poems. Selections]
Bastards of the Reagan era / Reginald Dwayne Betts.
pages cm
ISBN 978-1-935536-65-9 (pbk. : alk. paper)
I. Title.
PS3602.E8249B37 2015
811'.6--dc23
                    2015006031

This book is manufactured in the United States of America and printed on
acid-free paper.

Four Way Books is a not-for-profit literary press. We are grateful for the assistance
we receive from individual donors, public arts agencies, and private foundations.

This publication is made possible with public funds from the National Endowment for the Arts

NYSCA

and from the New York State Council on the Arts, a state agency.

[clmp]

We are a proud member of the Community of Literary Magazines and Presses.
Distributed by University Press of New England
One Court Street, Lebanon, NH 03766

Contents

Prologue

Elephants in the Fall

for Micah and Miles

I. Micah Michael Zamir Betts

November's flame in that year of hard sunsets,
        winter's plangency & days when
my insomnia courted cognac.
All our thoughts were beginnings,
& you became the roundness
that grew to a moon
above your mother's hips.
We waited without a name
for your wonder
& three days after your birth
twice named you after the uncle
you'll never meet. The names
questions: Micah, who resembles God.
Michael, who reminds us of who has gone too soon.
& we pronounced Micah as we wanted: Mekhi,
        because like the kid from *Clockers*,
we scrape fists and cuffs for the dreams of you.
& now, when on most days your body
is all blur & bustle—

Our song is how right we got it,
when the light from that moon spilled
out of your mother's belly, I tell
        you, you were smiling then,
as if you knew you were the first song
that found me worthy.

3

II. Miles Thelonious Betts

Named after the trumpet,
after the sound that comes from all
the hurt & want that leads a man
to turn his back to the world. We named
you after Monk, too,
because sometimes you have to
stack legends in a single body
already big enough for the sound of them
& we imagined that you gave us
a different tune,
a way to bang keys into each
other until our lives
filled with unexpected music.
I hear you call me daddy
in this land where my father's
name is sometimes another word
for grave, & I almost pause. It's the song

that wants to unravel me.
More crow than
swan, I've always been so much cage
& caged in. & all that changes when we square
the M. This old riff on a shotgun
marriage calls us back:
your mother's hand in mine & the shotgun is
what we aim at the world that threatens,

& I scoop you in my arms,
& you are calling us. Again.

Bastards of the Reagan Era

Elegy With a City in It

Many gone to grave: men awed
by blood, lost in the black
of all that is awful:
think crack and aluminum. Odd
what time steals,
or steals time: black robes, awful
nights when men offed in streets awed
us. Dead bodies sold news. What's real?
Murder cap & all that. The *Post* a jackleg reel
of it all: black death, awe.
Chocolate city awash in red:
500 bodies lost to morgues. Red

the gift of Glocks, red
sometimes a dark and awful
omen the best couldn't read.
Death reinvented when red
was the curse of men born black
and lost in a drama Reagan read
as war: crack vials and cash and red
in our eyes and we not still
with a pocket full of stones. Steel
in hands, and a god-awful
law aimed at stilling the red.
But ambition burns, makes men red

9

with a greed so damn real,
fattened by all that others read
in the *Post* about how real
it was in them streets. This reel
another *Scarface*, a flick that has awed
fools looking for something real
in the suicide of wakes, as if the real
is only what drowns: think Black,
Mario, Charles, they all blackened
the inside of a coffin, all real
flesh in that final moment, still
& nothing more, still

as men plotting on stealing
time from death, reeled
in from the street like dead fish. Steel
assured mutual destruction; steel
should have kept us safe. I read
the obits, those maps of death, still
as caskets holding men, still
as the bullet. Who is awed
by trouble? This awful
gristle & flesh torn by steel
turned into thunder. Ask Black,
dead in night's ruins. Bring out the black

ties the papers say. The black
hole is now the block. Steel
swallows men, spits them out black
eyed, spits them out black-
balled. Reagan's curse might be real,
might be what has niggas black-
mailing themselves, dancing in black-
face. Chocolate city red
under the scrutiny. Asphalt red.
When we heard about Black,
silence stole our voices, awful
silence, like death seemed odd,

& still when I sing this awful
tale, there is more than a dead black
man in the center, there is a city still
as all the bodies that make '86 real,
a city still, & awful, still & bloodied.

A Toothless Crackhead Was the Mascot

[An Outline for a Film]

A woman leans against a man who leans
against a brick wall watching cars stop like dead men
on this one-way street. Some dude glares
like O-Dog from *Menace*, his face towards some street
we'll never remember where a man some man
we'll never remember smokes white rocks from
an aluminum can that smells of death.

        This begins the concept of tragedy:
infinity the image of smoke running
from a soda can split & crumpled into a makeshift pipe.

There will be music because there is always music
& in this film it will be modern: a man rapping 'bout bricks
& all his homies in the pen & pouring out a little liquor. . . .
        Call it the story of a man pulled under by
a dollar's gravity.

Flash to the film within a film: reality TV, the young mother
of our star starring in another sad reality show calls
the Underground Railroad real, as in a train
that black people hopped on with one-way tickets.

At some point a photo of Malcolm &
his peering eyes staring out that window will flash in
the background as the young boys use a Gemstar razor to cut
up product. You be a fool to think
                    this ain't revolution.

We need a name: but we can't call this *Menace*
to the Hood or *Boys in Society* or no shit like that,
names already taken & used to make black men
rich peddling the prophecy of the doomed Negro
& broken Negress: Timberlands & Glocks & don't shoot
my baby cause that football contract. . .

& yes, there must be guns here, cause ain't nothing more
Shakespearean than death in the summer.

You see, a black boy says sorbet
justifies one thing—a black boy says get the fuck
out the car justifies another.

At the End of Life, A Secret

Everything measured. A man twists
a tuft of your hair out for no reason
other than you are naked, before him,
& he is bored with nakedness. Moments
ago, he was weighing your gallbladder
& then he was staring at the empty space
where your lungs were. Even dead, we still
insist you are an organ donor, as if something
other than taxes outlasts death. Your feet
are regular feet. Two of them, & there is no
mark to suggest you were an expert mathematician,
nothing that suggests that a woman loved
you when you died. From the time your body
was carted before him to the time your
dead body is being sent to the coffin,
every pound is accounted for, except 22 grams.
The man is a praying man & has figured
what it means. He says this is the soul, finally,
after the breath has gone. The soul: less than
$4,000 worth of crack—22 grams—
all that moves you through this world.

Bastards of the Reagan Era

I. Countdown to Armageddon

The Farm, this collection of dying men,
Is home for just another night. And now,
October's rust. Snow piles upon the dead.
Snow flattens the scarlet leaves of maple trees.
And crickets rule the black of night with song,
Or if you're like me you call it the noise
That wakes you from what troubles sleep. The guard
And his flashlight against steel bars. His voice
As low and tired as mine; authority
A gavel drop gave him makes me listen,
And I strip before this man who knows me by
A number, and I'm lost in shouts, and when
The chain-link belt and buckle wrap my waist
These nails begin to scrape the skin off my palms.
My eyes still sleep, the cuffs the bastard I
Pretend don't exist put on my flesh bite
And Peanut, from three cages down, he stare
Transfixed like some mad bullfrog into this
Sally port's opaque. I almost say:
"Shook one's afraid of sleep," but think his bid
Enough to let the dogs of his anger
Loose on the world, after these nights in a cell
Become nothing but more nights in a cell.
Outside the hawk reminds my bones of blocks
That straightjacket me in these cuffs, how want

For things had me on corners running wild
With bammas named Ray-ray, and Qwan, Dave: all
Of us like dogs in them streets, we were afraid
Is what I'm saying, all cliché and desire,
All ignorant of what madness did birth
The Swann Rds., Lancasters, and Oxford Knolls,
That damn near ruined me.

                                     I stand and stare,
Body trapped in this backcountry that bleeds
Men like leeches, body a stone that's kicked
From cell to godforsaken cell, each van
Ahead a sign, somewhere a light will flash,
And wake a man before he understands
His world has gone mad, every bus a ride
Another mile away from whatever
Circle of streets he claimed he owned. I have
Braved, for want of wild beasts, steel cages.
Carved my name on bunks and rafters. I fought
Grown men near double my age for a rep and now
This guard, he yanks against the chain so hard
I buck, then buckle, a man against a leash.
May God have mercy on all sleeping things!
This dark that fails to hide my trembling hands,
And all the cracked crowns with closed eyes in what
Passes for dreaming here. I'm boxed in,
Been here so long I sweat the funk of cells.

My mother wouldn't understand, not these
Half steps I take toward my bus escort
To hell. I graduated high school numb,
Already caged with a dead man rattling 'bout
My head, and get how these back roads will take
This body and, yes, bury it where I'm
Nobody, another man under barbed
Wire, count times, shakedowns, fistfights, shotguns, knives.

And when we walk into the cold air, I'm on
The corner, with darkness compassing my days.
All the currency I ever had was time,
Redundant gesture that it is. A waste,
That want for more. A waste, we half dozen,
Half shuffling, scuffed and nicked, on another
Schooner bound for some Sing Sing, for some
Angola, Folsom, Attica. They say
Armageddon been in effect. But let
Me tell you how this business began.

II. Bring the Noise

There is a limit to what facts can do.
A lefty with handles, a mean J, and white
Stones weighing down his pockets with hurt,
Jackson, at twelve, was a caution. Troubled, man.
Born on the wrong side of a twenty sac
His gift for the orange globe enough to keep

Those blooming tufts of yak smoke from his lungs
But not from clinging to skin, to clothes, to hair,
In places of business we called the block,
If we did any naming at all, because
Back then it was just outside, just around
The way, just where your kinfolks slept: just home.
I ran with him because of things
He knew: that recipe of death called crack,
The reasons why it would keep blooming black,
Which is all a way to say we were half-mad
With history, with thoughts of things we'd do,
Always half lost in a world where pistols caved
In dreams and embalming fluid ruined
A nigga's promise quicker than a bid.

You ask me why we figured the block would save
Us? We were in a cloud of rhetoric
And ganja smoke. The eighties a black cauldron
That christened Gator, Pookie, and how many
Others crackhead, fiend, crack baby, more?
Too black, too strong. We was lost in sounds:
The agitprop of Public Enemy,
The gunshots, sound of cocaine cooking, chrome
Mercedes-Benz hood ornaments ripped off
Cars and repurposed as pendants for chains.
We heard it all, and reveled in the worst.
In short: it takes a nation of millions and

All that. We thought revolutionary,
Sold crack and argued smoking the pipe was blues
For Reagan's babies. Scared of tomorrow,
We sculpted our identities from today.

III. Don't Believe the Hype

This voyage leaves our hero dead said Black.
He wasn't talking 'bout Jackson but could
Have been, Jackson in the dirt back where the dirt
Seem like a hustler's first reprieve. And Black,
So named by wit of youth who mocked his skin,
A Wonder Bread vanilla-toasted hue
That begged for moniker, for slang to say
He wore the veil, like us, despite his eyes
Near blue, he kept saying I didn't know why
I killed the dude, kept saying I felt threatened,
But we ain't know Monte, ain't know about
The threats of crazy niggas. Black ran out
With rain like fists pounding everyone and fear
Had him. They say he was a fucking fool,
The pistol smoking, Monte's blood and rain
Water washing over his sneaks. That's what
Black says, when someone asks him who will die,
Asks who the hero is. And for a sec
I think, imagine, Black bodied my boy,
And not some nameless young fool out for a rep.

But we all dead all dead all dead all dead
Already, lost and this a voyage from
Death to death, from godforsaken cell
To godforsaken cell and I can't stop
Thinking about before I owned these cuffs.

You remember *Raising Hell*? This my way
To admit fear to the men with me, to say
I'm drowning, too. And rope is memories, but
This van bends corners, slams on brakes and keeps
Me worrying today; and, six of ten
Of us are bastards of the eighties who
Have never heard Run rhyme. We are, again,
Close mouthed and staring dawn down. My eyes shut,
And damned if sleep doesn't leave me, again,
Explaining cuffs to closed eyelids.

IV. Night of the Living Baseheads

Most nights our energy was youth: hours
Out there after more hours out there. This was
The year of *Do the Right Thing*. Spike had us
On edge, near ready to toss a trashcan through
This city. Len Bias was dead. And we
Was lamping, stone cold lampin'. Pockets fat
Because we were entrepreneurs. And so
We figured: Every brother man's life is

Like swinging the dice. Why live so close to caskets?
After that Rockefeller wealth, a few
Got crushed by Rockefeller drug laws; locked
Slam up before the money flowed like piss
In a tenement hallway. Back then it was
Always winter, always cold in the street.
My mind rabid with want for equity,
For dukey gold chains, Jordans, more.
The hustle courted us. And we were down.
It'll take you to ruin moms would say,
As if disaster wasn't that damned place:
Those afternoons and all their sirens blare.
Maybe she knew that soon five sweet and love
Sized packs of crack would mean a flat
Nickel in a kaleidoscope of cells,
A mandatory minimum of years
Where home becomes God's nightmare. Our curse.

Back then the educated Negroes blamed
The Contras. They had seen reports, knew names:
Edén Pastora, Carlos Cabezas,
They had the Contras consorting with drug
Lords, plus Scarface ain't from Compton.
These Negroes who would have been Black Panthers,
Read Huey P and Cleaver, said the CIA
Funded a war with crack. Conspiracy,
The spook who sat beside the door, Hoover;

You couldn't blame them then, except Cleaver,
A fucking madman, actually wrote
He raped black women for practice, undercard
To raping white women, his bootleg play
For get-back born from bullshit ideas 'bout
An insurrectional against the man.
May God have mercy on fools and their victims!
I been a fool, too, but never did get
How niggas ran with him. Plus Hoover won,
And some say all we got was free breakfast.

Still if you listened back when someone said
To let a hundred flowers bloom, and you
Were watching when the martyrs, the Malcolms,
And Kings and Fred Hamptons fell, you might think of
How democracy, like communism, ends
In a body bag for the freedom fighters. Or
You might not care, you might have been like us,
Alive in the aftermath. You saw Rayful
Get locked and knew who the suckers would be,
(All we who fought for scraps we couldn't hold)
And still you posted on corners lost in this.

V. To the Edge of Panic

Some people say prison is the country
Where life is cheaper than anywhere else;
You wouldn't doubt that watching us take leave,

From dark to dark to Greensville where the last
Death waits for some. Virginia still a place
That will end you. The wrong fool's errand:
At your feet, some body. Black and you almost
Be straight, a decade, maybe two—a dead
White woman will have you slumped, biding time
Until your number called. And then you gone.

Our caravan three deep and black against
The wine-dark asphalt, and two of three
Are nothing but escorts: four uniformed
Shotguns (off safety) leading and flanking
Our coffle, all intent to keep us here,
And not wherever shackles and cuffs run
In this dead of morning, less than eighty miles
From where Nat Turner dug a hole and lay
For weeks. Virginia, something noose-like then
And some say still, except for all the shit
We did to land in this here hull and cul-
De-sac. The guard, he say "die, but don't run"
When one of us begin to cough his lung
Up in sleep. And this is ruin. Damn these chains!
This awkward dance I do with this van! Two-step,
My body swaying back and forth, my head
A pendulum that's rocked by the wild riffs
Of the dudes I'm riding with: them white folks know
You ain't god body, what you commune wine

And bread? Where you from son? Red lines?
To what Onion? My eyes two caskets though,
So the voices are sheets of sound. Our van as dark
Inside as out, and all the bodies black
And voices black too and I tell my God
If you have ears for this one, know I want
No part of it, no icepicks and no fears.
I don't say shit. I sing my dirge.
                                        This place,
The cracked and scratching vinyl seats, the loud
Loud talk of murder this and blanket fear
Around the rest, is where I'm most at home,
But it's beyond where prayers reach, a point
Something like purgatory. I lean back
And drift in sleep as someone says, his voice
All hoarse and jacked, all broken songbird-like
All revolutions end with an L-note.

VI. Caught, Can We Get a Witness

A grave: a place where men go trouble death,
This corner, prison, purgatory holds
My breath and body, fucks with my mind until,
Until the time becomes my coffin; we
Inherited a world wretched with crack,
A world beginning with a trek like this:
A van, the wine-dark asphalt, cuffs, the night

Of early morning and all that I can't
Imagine changing. Men around me chained,
Like me, and we all too damn comfortable
In cuffs, our journey long enough to think
About each nickel, dime and dub we sold.

Our caravan takes us from where men go
To die to where insane men go to ruin.
We got to Marion and shuffled, cuffed
And shackled; told to piss in a white box
Contraption I'd never seen. No running
Water, hands still wet with piss, then they
Handed us the sandwiches. Fuck them.

Inside, the van alive with talk about
The Onion, this wild place where we would be
Dumped like cargo from this schooner's bowels.
Three hundred years on that van, men tied to crimes
They committed when old age was so so far
Away. Conspiracy—they say explains
Our bodies borne into another thrall;
But here, we all recall the pistol's weight,
And how the gun in hand, the dope and crack
Turned some men into monsters, turned some men
To ghosts. The youngest here. . . man shit it's all
The same, same fucking thing, a narrative
That ends with cuffs around all wrists, again.

VII. Louder Than a Bomb

I wrote my cousin twice. First time to say
The world was never fair, then later cause
My father said he saw his pops come off
The Seventy, a bus that runs straight through
The city, past the Mecca, Howard U
And straight down Georgia Ave. A single head
Nod and they had talked more than your pops
To you or mine to me. Bastards, they call
Us, buried in our father's shadowed lives.
A toothless crackhead was the mascot. Block
A funeral. These series of cells the hell,
The purgatory from which I see the past.
The cats around me are on that dope talk,
Too young for prison, but they here. D boy
This, D boy that. Say Ricky Ross got it.
Say Rayful Edmonds a kingpin. Around
Us? Skeletons: all that drug money gave.
These cuffs are like a goddamned noose around
My neck. I peddled crack to pregnant women
And this cell is my reminder of the wages.
Rockefeller and Reagan, the NAACP
All wanted us away from corners, dead
Or jail but gone. I could tell you I changed
But history will haunt us all. My past
Almost a way to prep for this descent
To Red Onion, a prison carved inside
A mountain where black men go to die slow.

Narcotics left niggas null and void. Some
Will know this thing here true: when Huey's deal
Went up in smoke, the revolution dead,
Or dying when some cat in Oakland said
To Huey smoke inside a dime bag would
Make it all go away, what chance did we,
The rest of us with fathers brilliant, doomed
Like Huey have? I sold enough cocaine
To buy a legacy, but here, on this
My caravan to hell I am a man
With regrets, who just wants his body whole.

VIII. Security of the First World

Can't sleep for dreaming and in every dream
I'm cornered, damned again because the face
Before me bleeds; the boy I damn near killed
A crimson dawn returning me to my cuffs
As this, my caravan escort to where
The bones are buried pulls into the grave
Called the Onion, and all we see is gray:
The bricks, the doors, the buildings, overcast sky.
Then, why the kid beside me says I hope
This is the last stop? Naive so he thinks
Hell only has one layer, but we off
Of our voyage now and this here stop is to
Leave bodies, all of us doomed by what's worse.

If you imagine welcome was there when
We arrived you'd be wrong. When we stepped
Off the van we blended into the gray
Of everything else and guards barked orders
At us. The young among us still wanted
To be tough. To talk shit to guards.
I hear the where my food at CO and fuck
You punks as if it was nothing more than
The breeze washing against my skin in this
Thin mountain air that bites at skin and pride.
A stick, a twig beneath my foot near cut
Into the thin white soles of my state shoes.
I walk shackled into my latest home.
I may as well be a settler here, this cell
My homestead. You ask why they strip
Searched again. I will keep some secrets.

Old heads here say these chains and cells and walls,
State numbers, years and years and years upon
Years and years ain't nothing but Jim Crow.
They say it's slavery. The younguns damn
Near think it's normal though, a fucked up normal.
They have known cells like rivers and brown and
Black men returning to prison as if it's
The heaven God ejected them from. Me?
I'm praying for another Attica.
Even the guards driving us are black men,
All sharper than Al Sharpton on Sunday.

But if they'd spent another hour on the block,
If they'd never finished high school, if
They'd never left for basic training,
Maybe they end up here—shackled, cuffed
With us and the funk of a seventeen hour
Van ride across Virginia's jagged highways.

Green eyes, his voice another knife in this tomb,
Calls the van another cage. He talks
About a jail up North, so foul some days
The sewage seeped into the cells. Who cares?
Yes, this is hell to hell. Dostoevsky.
What did he say? You judge a nation by
Its prisons. Had he said you judge us with
Our crimes this van runs off the rail and back
Into the Atlantic from whence we came.
But see he didn't say that, and so what
Does all this say about America?
So many folks with control over our
Bodies. A public defender once explained
It perfect. He told me what we all know,
Said this is the business of human tragedy.

IX. Prophets of Rage

This dance we do, it borders on insane.
We all have names we let bravado mask:
Think Cassius Clay becoming Ali. Blame

This debt we pay to human guile on shame.
That's why Ramon became Ray-Ray, why Charles
Became Big Slim, then Chucky, Porkchop, Black;
Not Charles, nah never Charles, always in search:
Of room, escape, a way to run and claim
The blocks that buried us, launched us on this,
A flight from freedom. But I digress.
We were all running down demons with our
Chests out, fists squeezed to hammers and I was
Like them, unwilling to admit one thing:
On some days I just needed my father.

Crimson

When they found his body today,
all forty-seven of his years drowned
in a pool he paid for with blood, I thought
of my brother. He has life. The police cracked
Rodney King's head open before a live
audience. This is 1991 & the Bad Boys
from Detroit were in the Finals again, or will be
when June comes around & all around me shatters.
They say King had 59 fractures, bones brittle
brittle after that night when he became
why every young dude I knew shouted "Fuck
the Police." We only cursed what could kill us:
the day blood washed over the freshest pair of Timbs
on a Richmond street, those batons slam dancing
on King's head, my father's weary eyes, &
the money, all those thousands we spent trying
to resurrect a dead man with an appeal,
the millions spent making King rise again.
His name, my brother's, is Juvenile, or Juvie—but
no longer Christopher. This is what he tells me
the men he breaks bread with call him. Or called
him, a dozen years ago, before he, too, became
an old head, veteran of count time & shakedowns.
It's how they christen niggas who own their first
cell by sixteen—& because King took that ass
whupping four days before cuffs clanked around
Christopher's wrist that first time, back when he

was what they call on the run, when the news
came on, & we caught it halfway through, just
listening as we sweated the phone for news,
we saw King, & thought him Chris, my brother,
slumped under batons & boots, under the cops' blows.

For the City That Nearly Broke Me

A woman tattoos Malik's name above
her breast & talks about the conspiracy
to destroy blacks. This is all a fancy way
to say that someone kirked out, emptied
five or six or seven shots into a still warm body.
No indictment follows Malik's death,
follows smoke running from a fired pistol.
An old quarrel: crimson against concrete
& the officer's gun still smoking.
Someone says the people need to stand up,
that the system's a glass house falling on only
a few heads. This & the stop snitching ads
are the conundrum and damn all that blood.
All those closed eyes imagining Malik's
killer forever coffled to a series of cells,
& you almost believe them, you do, except
the cognac in your hand is an old habit,
a toast to friends buried before the daybreak
of their old age. You know the truth
of the talking, of the quarrels & how
history lets the blamed go blameless for
the blood that flows black in the street;
you imagine there is a riot going on,
& someone is tossing a trash can through
Sal's window calling that revolution,
while behind us cell doors keep clanking closed,
& Malik's casket door clanks closed,

& the bodies that roll off the block
& into the prisons and into the ground,
keep rolling, & no one will admit
that this is the way America strangles itself.

For the City That Nearly Broke Me

Knots like two dozen fists
sway with want from the boy's
keffiyeh, that black & white scarf
with its useless hands clopping
against the wind in protest,
against this boy & his somebody
lost, against their own swaying
in a dance the lost body has lost.
A boy. A somebody lost. A body bodied
in the lights of inauguration night
when every light in the city flared
with hope. Always losing, always
a boy left with a dozen weights,
small circles on strings pulling
his head down to the ground.
Downcast. Drop your bucket here
& make the city yours and all
that jive keeps him from running.
Escaping the pavement, where
bodies finally fall to rest.
The keffiyeh keeps him from
bucking against the wind,
hurtling himself to the Grey-
hound or Amtrak or I-95
with a book bag & hitched finger.
His head shrouded in the black
& white, the knots keeping

his eyes down as he traverses
neighborhoods with names like Third
World, with names like a nation
falling. & the coffin-voiced
boy is who God tells us he will
save, & so those swinging knots
must be a kind of redemption,
a way to see the bullets that bury
you, constantly, as if death is
the disguise hiding your wings.

Elegy With a RIP Shirt Turning Into the Wind

Some days, away from me,
the air turns & I pray
pistols into my hands, as if
there is a peace that will open
up with bullets, with the blucka
blucka blucka of a hammer's siren.
In the street, the boys play a game they call
throwback. It is football, every man
for himself as he weaves under
the wires above Mississippi
Avenue. The sneakers swinging
above his juking body like scythes
are fresh: Jordans, Air Force 1s & Chuck
Taylors singing death songs when
the wind blows hard enough.
Touchdowns are as rare as angels
& when the boy turns his body,
the RIP shirt slants against the wind,
& there is a moment when he is not
weighed down by gravity, when
he owns the moment before he crashes
into the other boys' waiting arms & they
all look like a dozen mannequins,
controlled by the spinning sneaker
strings of the dead boys above them.

For the City That Nearly Broke Me

Stress this: the lit end
of anything will
burn you. & that is just
just a slick way of
saying: running will
never save you. This
man's first son caved, fell
to the pressure, to
the barrel's indent
against his temple.
A body given
back to asphalt.
Stress this: we never
gave a fuck, not 'bout
Malik or how the
bullet didn't split
the air, but split those
edged-up, precise hairs
of his caesar, to save
the man the burden
of years fearing death.

For the City That Nearly Broke Me

Nothing here can be considered prayer,
not clasped hands, not heads bowed in abeyance,
not the screams that ratchet against the white
walls of this school. The students lean in,
swallowed by the noise they invent,
staring as two bodies prance around
each other like the shadows of God's hands
sparring with the world. & someone will die,
though not here, not this day, in this hall where
trauma clashes & breaks against silence.
The inevitable: the world reduced
to fists and the heads weaving. & fuck it
all as the mob of students and teachers
watching wonder what we hunger for
in the center of this ghetto gifted by
segregation & decades of racist housing
policies. Blood is the voice of an angel leaving
the body. So what are the two boys in
this hallway doing? Evicting angels that keep
us ruined in these bodies, forever
longing for a flight they refuse to give,
those winged bodies thrown from heaven.
I watch the boys fight. Most would call
the light-skinned kid pretty, & imagine
his life is good, despite the crack vials.
& maybe it's true—but pretty won't save
anyone here, where currency is blood,
where pretty has failed everyone, even
cherubim, out to leave us to this world.

For the City That Nearly Broke Me

In streets that grieve our silence, children die,
they fall to bullets & asthma, they fall
into each other's arms as mothers watch on.
& there is a secret to why the small boy
can step into the street & no one notices
as it swallows him whole, a mathematics
for the hold that Newports have on men
struggling with child support & probation.
These eyes sifting through madness, that
avalanche of laughter ringing inside a
broken man's head. You explain the voices.
You explain Khalif's five-year sentence for
possession, for believing that there's a pension
plan for the pusherman, for Mayfield's hero
turned skinny jeans-wearing teen. This street
inhales Du Bois. Inhales Shawn, too. Men left out
of imagination's prophecy. Wading in the water.
Men that slept with the city's youngest girls,
believing virginity a talisman that would
protect them against death—men who still died.
& there are names. I'm only talking about Ray-Ray,
& Mario, Damon & Mike—people we called
bereft, a fancy name for being in a fight with God
& the Devil, for a small child begging
for his mother, who is not here, who too
has been flooded by the suicide of asphalt.
Newports & fried chicken. There is this sadness
in the world when all the stereotypes seem true.

A calling for a block party, where men in
the streets stop pretending to be Crispus Attucks,
stop thinking one more nameless man
can get named eternally after a bullet bursts
through his skin, through the tattoo that marks him.
I'm here, another body navigating what mothers'
fear. There is nothing you see while cruising
down the Ave. that explains what's in the hooded
head that stares into your car. But he knows
the revolution starts with whatever is left
after WIC checks get cut. When I tell my brother
I'm hustling, I mean it. Damn it, I mean it.

For the City That Nearly Broke Me

My lover is walled into silence in your borders,
no my lover is the wall of silence that defines
your avenues. You want to know about desperation?
About the way the seams of everything come apart?
There is an alleyway near Mississippi Ave
that once became evidence. An officer's fingertip,
the trigger he pressed gentle just a reminder that people
die within your silence. There are rags here.
& if I hold this woman's hand & start to talk
of beauty, she becomes the chaos of early pregnancy.
You want me to imagine what?—Some days
all I notice are the potholes & the cracks in pavement
that say something is threatening to swallow this city whole.

Elegy Ending With a Cell Door Closing

& the Judge told him to count
the trees in the parking lot
where there were only cars. Zero.
The same number of stars
you could see on a night in the city.
& the judge told him the parking lot will
be filled with trees, oaks & spruces
& pines & willow trees & grass & maybe
horses before he smells the city
on a Sunday afternoon; & another word
for this story is azalea, the purple bouquet
his mother buried her face against,
her skin another purplish bruise—
he pleaded guilty, & in the courtroom
he washed his hands against the air,
as if to say fuck everything;
imagine, he had no hair on his face
that afternoon & he'd never held a razor,
except inside his mouth, the best weapon
a man could ask for unless you lost
the first fight he'd see in prison,
a baseball bat turning the razor under
the bad man's tongue into a kind of prayer—
made the man wash the air with his hands,
too, & then everyone knew the washing
was a kind of suicide, & everyone knew
there would never be trees in that parking lot—
that the chubby kid who a whole

neighborhood called Big Boy would lose
every memory he's had in the wildfire of his
mind folding itself around a rusted bar.

Legacy

after George Jackson

Because something else must belong to him,
More than these chains, these cuffs, these cells—
Something more than Hard Rock's hurt,
More than remembrances of where men
Go mad with craving—corpuscle, epidermis,
Flesh, men buried in the whale of it, all of it,
Because the so many of us mute ourselves,
Silent before the box, fascinated by the drama
Of confined bodies on prime-time television,
These prisons sanitized for entertainment &
These indeterminate sentences hidden, because
We all lack this panther's rage, the gift
Of Soledad & geographies adorned with state numbers
& names of the dead & dying etched on skin,
This suffering, wild loss, under mass cuffs,
Those buried hours must be about more
Than adding to this surfeit of pain as history
As bars that once held him embrace us.

For the City That Nearly Broke Me

He told you he didn't believe
in the colors you draped me in,
didn't believe in the shadow's
black or the silver bang
of the prettiest pistol he ever saw.
He wanted everything
you offered the boys he knew
died in your arms. He wanted
flame & the intensity of regret.
& damn if you don't give
a man any & everything he asks for.

For the City That Nearly Broke Me

it's all counter
intuitive,
 breathing bullets,
walking the street
 & staring down
the corner's eye,
all minding your
 contemplations,
remembering
thug as label
         inaccurate,
as misnomer;
 the homeless man not
as failed timing:
 all not breaking
the ground with your body
to be naked
with some clothes on,
 all some savage
believing, all
 knowing some
say prison
         is nothing more
than a long way home.

For the City That Nearly Broke Me

You—all reflux & reflex.
Abandoned. All mystery divined.
All misplaced haymakers. Men
in your shadow gamble with horns
& halos. Fat Gary. Brandon.
Oatmeal. Peanut. The names
true as the drums they got shouted
over, names etched into recordings,
pitched like coins into a pool
of piss. Bodies just past your borders.
Trapped between Hennessy &
a hard place, some craved collapse. Pistol in hand,
pistol in hand. Some craved collapse. Craved
an abridged distance. Tooley Street,
Oxford Knolls, Lancaster Square
all laced with echo.
Displaced residents even then,
in the 90s, late 80s, filling out
land people once farmed.
Your borders were between JYB
& Illmatic, Midnight Marauders
& Trouble Funk. Nobody believes
in plea bargains, so you plead
to the nuance of running away. Talk
about hunger & the absence of it.
Talk about them dudes on the roof

talking about the Library of Congress.
Talk about never owning a damn thing,
& then talk about us. To be so young,
so full of wanting to be tough. To be trouble.

The Invention of Crack

I.

Dark alliance. Crack smoked over this backdrop:
CIA seal, Contras. So much heavy weight.
How birds fly? How millions turn into guerrilla props:
AK-47s, & all else. White smoke. Rocks. The dead & dying.
Gary Webb's tale of two horrors: Contra & crack.

Mr. Speaker, what is most
frightening about crack
is that it has made cocaine
widely available. . . Mr. Speaker,
I am afraid that the crack epidemic
will only get worse.

I wish to bring to the attention
of our colleagues an article,
"Extra-potent cocaine: use
rising sharply among teenagers."
Confirms what many of us in the Congress
who have the responsibility of reviewing
federal drug abuse policy
have known for some time;
that the availability of "crack" —
cocaine in its purest state—
at low street prices will only
expand the abuse of cocaine nationwide.

Black man say crack will ruin. Senator Black Elect say scourge
& scourges & look behind the words & you know he knew
"there is always a prison for them." This post Rockefeller,
after Carmona got laced with a life sentence for a hundred
dollars worth of heroin. Ain't many black folks in Congress.
Keep saying Reagan did it. Black man say Reagan did it.
Reagan say look at the paper, the bodies in the street. Rangel
says scourge & you vote for him again & again & again
& the pen is still filled with the bodies. Ain't no conspiracy here.
Hand to hands scared him. Black man watching the projects
turning into a war zone. Probably thought if no one notices
the zombies in the street he should. Don't tell me he trafficked
in the New Jim Crow too. Rangel says scourge. All these years,
all these years & the bodies in prison & we done
stop counting but I know what he told the papers:
We'd stopped counting. Stopped counting how many babies
lost their mothers to the pull of smoke running from aluminum.
We had. Stopped. Counting. Mr. Senator was out to duck ruin.
Ours. It seems. You think we counted our lost? Lost
pounds, lost brothers? All the women who bartered
with the dirt their knees gathered in the dusk?

> *The newest scourge on the streets*
> *is a frightening low-cost substance*
> *called crack. This form of cocaine,*
> *which users freebase, has been proved*
> *lethal time and again, and it's responsible*

for an alarming number of episodes of death
and injury in recent weeks.

II.

Nickel bag, Dime bag, Eight ball:

> We invented a way for niggas to be
> good at math. Call me crackhead, call me
> fiend, but I know my Daddy's name
> is what I tell them young boys,
> even as they wave me on to the spot
> where a kid my son's age passes out rocks.

Jesus, some of us still be praying with aluminum between
our lips. All our music reduced to something clever to say
about dope. Call it white lady. Call me snowman. Say
I move avalanches. I drought the city. From the first to the fifth
I got it all back. Crown me rap star. If I ain't a hustler
what you call that. I was just trying to feed my babies.
Move weight. Fly birds. Call me Ricky Ross. Call me
Dopeman. Pusherman. He who gots bricks. Move that dope.
This, all of it, the abyss where men come to die. & the rest
of America goes to watch. Where Rangel at? Ha ha. & they
still say whitey did it. I been had my money on the man
that stay in office, that gets in office, that suits up to go
prosecute, that suits up to go defend. I say they did it. What?
Watch when the city went to ruins. Inheritance ain't nothing

but memory. When the mayor & the reporters smoking too,
why we the only ones in jail? Where all those men who dreamed?
They keep saying in the 80s a Smokey, Teddy, Luther would have
Crooned to a crack pipe. We pray that Thou wilt grant, O Lord,
Whatever will that will bury what brought smoke, crystalline
white rocks to our streets.

> Rayful. Freeway Ricky. Supreme. Everyone wanting
> to be Escobar. A proliferation of bodies enlarged
> by cameras. Philargyrist: lover of money, antecedent
> to Andre 3 stacks, to all those pockets full of stones.
> They say where the earth has no water there is a man
> craving the shiny glimmer of a nickel, or of the ragged
> end of pipe in their mouths. 1980 something.
> Corposant & corpse. Or fuck your hearse.

III.

It take a nation of millions to hold
us back? Well they got that. We got that too.
Hands around our throat. Before you suffocate
your own fool self. Father forgive. . .

So the penitentiaries are barrels full of
children running away from Jake, Bodine,
5-0, all these names for the same dance. On the Run.

& watch when the researchers come, notebooks in hands
writing about the dispossessed. About the clean & dirty.
Their idioms of death & whatnot. King me muthafucka,
they say when the research drops. Expert on the Negro
Problem. They become oracle & insight. & we get all
the dead bodies around us. Say so many people died one year
the District was worse than Vietnam. Per capita they say. Per
capital. Meaning all the capitals in the world was better to be in than
here where Sam did go to college no matter what the news say.
& he came back & paid rent like all these good folks
with dogs & shit do now. Talk about the victor writes history.

The Reagan Era, the cocaine era, them boys from Dunbar
could hoop is what I mean to say. All the dope gets in
the way though. Me remembering their story
a bag at a time & ain't none of them get high.
My uncle caught touchdowns for Bladensburg,
where his story. My aunts ain't get high, my mom,
where their story? All their history buried in the
narrative of the shooter, of the one pitching them kilos.
We buried a nation inside the lungs
that fill with smoke, & the smoke smothers the nation,
& the nation is the small child crying in the corner,
& the barrels are filled with crabs....

Joseph E. Lowery, president
of the Southern Christian Leadership
Conference, urges blacks to turn in
drug pushers regardless of race.
"We are devastated spiritually
and emotionally by what crack
and other drugs are doing to our people,"
he said, "Drugs represent the new
lynch mob that is more effectively killing
our people than the old lynch mobs."

Always that same hurt,
    You think a man don't
Know what a high can do?
    Flattened an entire city
Block a few guns did—
    I tell my shadow we made
It all possible. You know
    Getting high ain't the move,
But ask someone who's been
    There, shit feels like coming
For days, that's what they
    Said about heroin—crack,
It feels like God has dropped
    A piece of heaven behind
Your eyelids. After that, all
    You want is to be that close
To an angel again.

for Poochie, Charlie, Donovan & Frankie

They mourn together, drown
        with the rest of their brothers
in cuffs. Say they were lost: chaos
        with a bullet; say there was no rest
from being hard. & that they,

all four restless, ran into the night
        with guns, not prayers.
Say they thought they couldn't
        afford rest, not in that Akron.
Who, cuffed to the hood, rests? Say

they felt power: The burners
        made folks take them serious, burned
flashing steel into nightmares,
        ruined rest.
Troubled their belief in God. Shattered air.
        They didn't kill though.
Just waved guns in the air

& their voices thundered,
        & rooms became still.
The city didn't rest when it started.
        Say violence fattened the air—
& they were all so damn young.
        Call them heirs

of cell doors clanking closed; call
        them lost inside prison
with violence, again, in the air. 50 witnesses.
        The lady said, "I was praying."
Poochie knows. The lady says,
        "I was praying

for the boys." Their eulogies
        were there, in the air. They should've
said guilty in song, made a hymnal
        of it—a plea,
started praying in court. Say
        the gavel burned them,

pounding gavel more threat
        than any burner. They learn
time in prison, learn the calendar &
        confined air. They wake
young & bound by count time & chow call,

burning in a purgatory
        where there is no rest.
& their lives: music, that same
        melody—,
where prison is the imitation
        of life. No burner saves
a man from time. & locked

up is to be lost.
        Decades, love, the smell of Akron.
What isn't lost?
        Frankie says he was far-gone.
Say that made the burner
        the natural choice. Say prison
teaches you to pray,

to fall down on knees & start
        whispering as if prayer
is the one thing missing. Maybe it is.
Say prayer is prison's gift. A way
        to hunger. A way to burn

a shout on your brain. A way
        to live in the world
without being prey.
A fifty-year sentence buckles
        a man's knees into prayer.

Charlie say, "Only thing
        matter is where you at."
This air, he means, will suffocate
        most, change those not preyed
upon, ruin those broken by

loving the world in prayer.
    If they couldn't rest on the block,
they couldn't rest
        in prison, not when every day
they scuffled to wrest

hope from concrete & carceral. Say
        there is only prayer,
as if speaking to the unseen is
        a way to not feel lost.
Imagine ten consecutive
        twelve-year bids, imagine

being lost in that. They walked
        rec yards with muscles
flaring, lost to what awaited.
        Imagine, time is God & prayers
to her are answered by victim's cries.

What lost would save them:
        not safety, not sanity, not time lost—
so what they were born
        where factories closed & the burners
they held made them
        legends. Say you can be lost
in what gives you a name.

Ask them, they know Akron
      is lost
inside all that prison has given
      & snatched. The air
of the city didn't drift to rec yards,

there they breathed air
      at the crossroads where some
men have to go back, lost,
      looking for they self. Ask Charlie,
Donovon, Frankie, about rest,
      ask Poochie. Ask every man in
every prison. There is rest

in the grave. Pressed against
      tomorrow, prison is what the rest
of us have nightmares about.
      They want forgiveness.
They're lost in the aftermath of what
      made them infamous. Maybe
praying

is the only real option. Maybe
      only God can forgive what burns
a man's history, forgive
      that smoke wafting in the air.

For Shawn, & Malik, Quan, & Moe—
their names all echo, legacy
of Maryland Ave., Georgia Ave.,
& Alabama Ave.— names robbed
of flesh by callow boys (all peach
fuzz & pistols) ruined by
a rack of streets that bleed white chalk.
For David, Craig, Amir & Black—
who sought to shout in time with Wink's
pocket of sound in dark & wild
night space: the Ibex, Black Hole, those
dank clubs where bodies sweated night.
Wink's progeny, conga players
banging out time on flattened globes,
that mean pocket of scars filling
coffins & classrooms. What will you
say to gunmen? Their names still
carving your landscape? Shawn, Malik,
DaQuan—names scarred by hurt. What will
you say about so much chaos,
about the graffiti, those names
& young faces tatted on shirts
& jackets, those clear closed caskets.

For the City That Nearly Broke Me

He heard your rumors, caught
the words a mother's ear
abhors, the stories there,
the wounds of Barry Farms
& Trinidad, those blocks
& bodies, Simple City
& Stanton Terrace, blocks
& bodies—this Black Hole,
this Capital, this home
of hurt, percussion, beat
downs; this home of love,
them twenty sacks of boat,
the Bullets & Bernard's
half-busted knee. You gave
the crossover, the hands
up, the stutter step
& step back. You gave them
the Mecca—Howard U,
that frontispiece staring
a casket down. You owned
the pocket, the rhythm
that left him & his boys
inside your borders, deep.
& they: all shouts, all riot,
all Homer Ave., Swann Rd.,
& Rushtown, all so much
wanting over bass
& snare. & you, you gave
& savored all that hurt.

What We Know of Horses

I.

& when my brother says Swann Rd.
is the world, he ignores boarded
vacants, broken windows—this place's
shattered glass? He tells me,
"Believe the world is tenement house,
a pocket full of stones, a world
of ghosts, & what's left of ash &
smoke after each inhale." I visit now
that a prison cell holds his world.
Dead men circle every block
we know, thread this world
with quotes from psalms, "the sorrows
of death embrace me," "some trust
in chariots and some in horses."
They embrace metaphor, disbelieve
gravity, breathe in a haunted world.
& what of my brother? Running
these streets, he was a horse—
graceful, destined to be
broken. Why admire horses?

II.

Why compare everything fast
& beautiful to horses?
My daddy's generation had a saying
for men lost in the world,
it was true of my uncle, my cousin—
men strung out on horse,
chasing the dragon, shivering
with the memory of that stallion
gone postal in their veins—
called them lost in place,
with cities buried inside them—horses
inside them stampeding.
My brother put his faith in horse,
& there is no map to find him now.
He tells me he inhales
the funk of men doing life
& knows he is in hell,
that he has dug his grave
amongst bricks that embrace him.
He—exile, with only rusted iron
& bricks bracing his two hundred pounds.

III.

Who admits this cage embraces
him? "History is written
on the back of the horse" broken
by the world. We all in prison now.
I stare at this man, my kin
ruined by embracing
night. Call this place a horse collar,
& watch how it cuts into skin,
how the leather embraces
all of our necks. Even as a visitor
behind plate glass I brace
myself for cuffs. This not Swann
Rd., this burden placed on me,
these memories of courtrooms
& the places where bodies were found.
& still, I want to stop & embrace
my brother, to hold him close
& pause to inhale the scent of prison,
to tell him what I smell, what I inhale,
is still the body of a man.

IV.

How can a man inhale
so much violence & not change?
I light my Newport, inhale.
Think on how his voice has changed.
My man, now a feral horse
wearing kick chains: unable to sleep,
always on guard, inhaling
the air for prey, as if he is still
the predator, as if he can inhale
death & keep on living. Death
the elephant in this world.
I imagine the other men here, all
in a world filled with a casket's aftermath.
How much grief can you inhale?
My brother tells me he prays
at night, he wants to leave this place.
But we know all his wild hours placed
him in this mural of blood.
His hunger placed him in C-block,
Cell 21. It suffocates
& nothing replaces time.

V.

"You okay in here?" I ask.
But he's in a place
only he knows. When he walks
away he embraces
the kind of rage I fear. A man
killed a man near him, placed
on a gurney & rushed
down a sidewalk. Dead
in a place where no one gives
a fuck if you're breathing.
To be a horse galloping away
is what I want for him,
he wants horse trundling through
his scarred veins. Prison
has taken the place of
freedom, even in his dreams.

VI.

& I know, this is not a "world
where none is lonely." & I know,
he is lost to the world,
& I know he believes this:
"I shut my eyes and all the world
is dead," & I know that there is
still a strip, a place
that he believes is the world:
Swann Rd., where he can inhale
& be free. Sometimes his cuffs
are on my wrists & I embrace
the way they cut, as if I am the one
domesticated, a broken horse.

Acknowledgments

I gratefully acknowledge the editors of the following journals and magazines in which these poems, sometimes in different versions, first appeared:

Folio, The Kenyon Review, Muzzle Magazine, New England Review, The New York Times Magazine, The Normal School, Pluck Magazine, Poetry, River Styx, San Pedro River Review, and *Tidal Basin Review.*

My deepest gratitude also to the Radcliffe Institute for Advanced Study at Harvard University and the Poetry Foundation for their generous support and encouragement. Further, my thanks go out to Bill Henderson and the Pushcart Prize editors for selecting "What We Know of Horses" and "Elegy With a City in It" for Pushcart Prizes.

This one's for all my kinfolks: One way or another it's always for my Moms. Grandma. Aunt Linda. Aunt Tricia. Aunt Violet. Aunt Bonnie. Uncle Tom. Aunt Pandora. & Uncle Darren. For Kareem: welcome home. Jamaal. Nikki. Ramon. Delonte. Kalisha. Andre. Mak. Kiya. Marquita. Pebbles. Josh. Aje'. Nathan. Junior. Roc. Jeremiah. Joshua. Omar. Kim. Brian. & the rest of the Worthington family. My Pops. My little brother Kenneth. My sisters: Jeannette, Jac, & Jennifer. The three cats who got my back regardless: Marcus, Tony, Torrence.

To the poets and writers who helped make this happen: Cathy Chung: for being my first reader. John Murillo: my executive producer. Haven't written a book yet without you going cover to cover with me. Nancy Schwalb and the DC Creative Writing Workshop. Martha Rhodes. Randall Horton, Marcus Jackson, Tayari Jones, Chimamanda Adichie. Uzo Iweala. Ernesto Mercer. Brian Gilmore. TSE. Reginald Gibbons. Gaby Calvocoressi. Heather McHugh.

Honorée Jeffers. The entire Cave Canem. To Ross White and the Grind. &, always, for the lives that inspired these riffs. All these poems carry the memories of the men & women who watched me grow into a man. For Absolut, Juvie, and all the cats that know Shahid from way back when.

Finally, this is for Terese, Micah, and Miles. Because some don't understand that black love is black wealth, but we do.

Reginald Dwayne Betts is a husband and the father of two sons, a writer, and a poet. His first collection of poems, *Shahid Reads His Own Palm*, won the Beatrice Hawley Award. Betts's memoir, *A Question of Freedom: A Memoir of Learning, Survival, and Coming of Age in Prison*, was the recipient of the 2010 NAACP Image Award for nonfiction. His writing has also led to a Pushcart Prize, a Ruth Lilly Fellowship, and a Soros Justice Fellowship. In addition to his writing, Betts serves as the national spokesperson for the Campaign for Youth Justice and was appointed to the Coordinating Council of the Office of Juvenile Justice and Delinquency Prevention by President Barack Obama. He is currently a student at the Yale Law School.